Rapurrzel

by Liza Charlesworth
illustrated by Kelly Kennedy

SCHOLASTIC

New York ★ Toronto ★ London ★ Auckland
Sydney ★ Mexico City ★ New Delhi ★ Hong Kong

No part of this publication may be reproduced, stored in a retrieval system, or transmitted in any form or by any means, electronic, mechanical, photocopying, recording, or otherwise, without written permission of the publisher. For information regarding permission, write to Scholastic Inc., Attention: Permissions Department, 557 Broadway, New York, NY 10012.

ISBN 978-0-545-68631-0

Copyright © 2011 by Lefty's Editorial Services

All rights reserved. Published by Scholastic Inc.
SCHOLASTIC, LET'S LEARN READERS™, and associated logos are trademarks and/or registered trademarks of Scholastic Inc.

12 11 10 9 8 7 6 5 4 3 2 1 14 15 16 17 18 19/0

Printed in China.

Once upon a time in the kingdom of Kittypaws, there lived a queen who loved cats. She had fluffy cats. She had striped cats. She had cats with bright blue eyes.

"The finest cats belong to me,
And that is how it will always be," she said.

The cats roamed freely through the queen's castle. They ate the fanciest fish. They slept on the softest pillows. They were the finest cats in the kingdom, until one day . . .

. . . in a tiny cottage, down a twisty lane, a very special kitten was born. The kitten belonged to a kind basket maker named Steve.

The kitten had green eyes and golden fur. She also had a very, very, very long tail. The kitten looked at Steve and purred.

"What a sweet purr," said Steve. "I shall call you Rapurrzel."

At first, having such a long tail was tricky for Rapurrzel. She kept getting tied up in knots!

But as Rapurrzel grew, she discovered she could do great things with her extra-long tail. She could jump rope. She could swing. She could even write notes to Steve.

Life was sweet until the day the queen went for a little ride. Down the twisty lane bumped her royal carriage. Then she saw an awesome sight! Behind a tiny cottage was the most beautiful cat in the world.

And the cat had a very, very, very long tail.

"What an incredible creature!" said the queen. "I simply must have her."

Quick as a wink, she snatched Rapurrzel and drove home.

The queen locked Rapurrzel in the tippy-top of the tallest tower.

"Now you will never escape," she said. "And no one will ever find you."

Rapurrzel did not like the tower one bit. It was cold and dark. And she missed Steve. Steve missed Rapurrzel, too.

"I will search every corner of the kingdom until I find my beloved cat," he vowed.

Years passed, but the two friends never gave up hope of finding each other. Then, one day, Rapurrzel climbed into the tower window for a little catnap. Not surprisingly, she dreamed of Steve.

The dream made Rapurrzel so happy she began to purr. The purrs drifted down to the ground like pretty rose petals. The guards heard them. The queen heard them. And Steve heard them.

"That sounds just like Rapurrzel," he said.

Steve followed the purrs to the castle. Then he looked up—way up! In the tallest tower was a cat. Could it be Rapurrzel? There was only one way to find out.

"Rapurrzel, Rapurrzel, let down your tail,
And I will climb it without fail!" shouted Steve.

Rapurrzel woke up and looked down—way down! It was Steve! He had come to rescue her. *Thump . . . Bump . . . Wump!* She dropped her tail.

Steve grabbed the golden tail. He climbed and climbed until he reached the tippy-top of the tallest tower.

"My long-lost cat!" exclaimed Steve. "I can't wait to take you home."

"Purrrrrrrrr!" replied Rapurrzel.

"I think I'm going to be sick!" said the queen.

In a jealous rage, she burst into the room and hissed:

"The finest cats belong to me,
And that is how it will always be!"

Then the queen tried to grab Rapurrzel. But, quick as a wink, the clever cat tied her up.

"Let me go!" cried the queen.

"Only if you promise to unlock the door," said Steve. "And in return, Rapurrzel will come back to visit you."

At first, the queen refused. But the friendship between the man and the cat melted her icy heart. So she opened the door.

The queen led the two friends down a long, long, long staircase to freedom.

"I'm sorry," she said.

"We forgive you," said Steve.

"Meow," said Rapurrzel, which meant, *I can't wait to curl up inside one of Steve's baskets.*

After that, the queen invited Steve and Rapurrzel over for weekly play dates with her pampered pets. They jumped rope. They ate fancy fish. They took cozy catnaps.

And everyone in the kingdom of Kittypaws lived a purr-fect life forevermore.

Comprehension Boosters

1. Retell this story in your own words.
2. Can you think of five great words to describe Rapurrzel? How about the queen?
3. Why did the queen lock Rapurrzel in the tallest tower of her castle?
4. What important lesson did the queen learn?
5. What happens *after* everyone lives happily ever after? Turn on your imagination and tell a story about it!